Microcosm Publishing is Portland's most diversified publishing house and distributor with a focus on the colorful, authentic, and empowering. Our books and zines have put your power in your hands since 1996, equipping readers to make positive changes in their lives and in the world around them. Microcosm emphasizes skill-building, showing hidden histories, and fostering creativity through challenging conventional publishing wisdom with books and bookettes about DIY skills, food, bicycling, gender, self-care, and social justice. What was once a distro and record label was started by Joe Biel in his bedroom and has become among the oldest independent publishing houses in Portland, OR. We are a politically moderate, centrist publisher in a world that has inched to the right for the past 80 years.

Have you ever been in a raunchy mood? I hope so, cuz otherwise you're not human. And a zine-reading bot is the kinda idea that blows my mind. But have you ever gotten in a raunchy-ass mood thtat you couldn't break out of? Even if the original precipitating event was totally legit, you're exhausted of being controlled by it? You're ready to move on if only for the sake of your own sanity?

Paul Ekman (yeah, the guy *Lie To Me* is based on… he wrote a book called *Emotions Revealed*) says there's a huge difference between an emotion and a mood. I talk about this in my book *Unfuck Your Brain* and in other zines so forgive me if you have heard this a trillion fucking times.

An **emotion** is information about a specific circumstance that helps you make a decision on how to react and helps you store a specific memory about that event so you know how to react in the future.

A **mood** is an emotion that has been carried over from that specific situation and is now coloring most of what you say and do. It becomes this thing that we just can't seem to shake out of, or shift.

This doesn't suck when we are in a good mood. But being Admiral PissyPants for days (weeks, months, years) on end is no bueno. It's one of those situations where you have settled into a neg groove that you can't seem to shake.

Your people have told you *"Ugh, just get over it!"* You've told YOURSELF *"Fucking SERIOUSLY, get OVER yourself."* But the getting over it part isn't fucking happening, is it?

Breaking a mood takes concerted effort. Cartoon mice and birds aren't going to do your chores and make you a dress so you can head out to the ball. You're going to have to actually focus on what's going on and change shit for yourself. If you're reading this, I'm guessing it's cuz you're ready. And the good news is this is not Macho Grande. You are allowed to get over it.

(Bonus points for if you got that reference…congratulations for being one of about thirty people who actually saw *Airplane* II.)

This is the official Dr. Faith recipe for success. This is also where if I was a regular self-help writer I would say something like "Proceed At Risk Of Regaining Your Happiness" or some-such bullshit. But yeah, even typing that, even with total sarcasm font activated, made me throw up in my mouth. Since I'm nowhere near a regular self-help writer, let's say we are gonna board the train to FuckThatVille because we have better things to do than the shit we're doing now.

1) What story are you telling yourself about this situation?

We think in stories, communicate in stories, and live in stories. Humans are storytelling creatures. We even tell ourselves stories in our sleep and call it dreaming. Stories are clearly a fundamental human need. And moods are set by the stories we are telling. What's your story? *I was wronged, fucked over, dumped upon?*

This was unfair and I'm the hurt and wounded party? No one is worth anything? I'm not worth anything?

Be brutally fucking honest right now. What's the story that you keep living out that is keeping you from moving on? Write the story out, say it out loud, own that this is the story that you've taken as truth (at least up until now).

2) What's a new *just-fucking-possible* and *doesn't-suck-quite-so-bad* story?

I do a lot of training in cognitive behavioral therapy (CBT), since it's the mode of treatment the governing bodies love best in the state I live in. Which is cool, cuz even though I don't think it's the be-all end-all of therapeutic practice, there is a lot from CBT I use on a regular basis. Including this: Ask yourself, is your story (or thought, as they say) accurate and is it helpful?

A lot of people think CBT means changing your thoughts like everything is actually just-fucking-fine and you're a dumbass who doesn't realize it. And no, of course that isn't the case. CBT makes the case for having a rational perspective. Sometimes what we are thinking isn't accurate...it's coming from our past histories or other fucked-up messages we have gotten over the years. And sometimes, sadly, it's completely **accurate**. I've worked with kids with severe trauma histories. What they said about their abusers was always a hard-core truth.

But this is where the second part comes in. Your story isn't always **helpful.** Telling a story that keeps you down, no matter how true, doesn't do you any more favors as telling yourself a story that is complete bullshit.

So, an example.

Original story: *"My mom is a druggie who won't even get clean to get custody of me back because she cares more about heroin than about me"*

New story: *"My mom has a seriously fucked-up addiction. She doesn't have the capacity right now to be the mom I need her to be because she is living in that addiction. This is about her and her illness, this isn't about me and the person I am. It doesn't mean I'm unlovable or unimportant. It does mean I'm not going to be able to have a relationship with her right now, though. That I'm going to have to take care of myself, respect myself, make different choices than she made, and find other people in my life who do see me for what I'm worth."*

See the difference? It isn't about trying to blow smoke and sunshine up your own ass, but about stopping the tape you've been playing that is keeping you from moving on. It's a perspective shift that gives you back your value in the present and hope in the future.

A story that's kept you stuck in a raunchy mood is likely not accurate or helpful. I'm not saying you have to actually believe it yet, but what might a different version just possibly look like? Talk that one out.

Write it down. What makes it different? What does even the hope that it might be true feel like?

3) **We either win or we learn.**

I dated a football coach a while back. Football coach in *Texas,* mind you. He'd had kids that went pro, *Friday Night Lights* all the way. He started out hating this expression (it's a classic Dr. Faith-ism)...because his motto was you either win or you *win.* No losing, no learning. Just winning. Then pizza. But something shifted in him. Because we don't always win (duh). We can't. So we can turtle up or we can learn from the experience and not do that shit again. And if losing pisses us off, we missed out on a huge learning opportunity. We learn far more from failure than success. A pain in the ass but a seriously truthy truth.

Football Coach Dude found this expression coming out of his mouth one Friday night. The team took a loss...and he saw that loss as a mechanism to learn some new skills on the field rather than as a Taylor

Swift "Shake It Off" moment. His fellow coaches said he was creeping them out and needed to break up with the therapist chick...but out on the field the next morning they went. And they learned. And beat the shit out of the other team next time they played each other.

So you got your shit stomped into a mud hole. What did you learn that you are going to carry forward in life? What did you learn about certain situations or certain people? What did you learn about yourself and your bad-ass capacity for survival?

4) Grant yourself the serenity.

You've heard the serenity prayer, I know. Even if you aren't in recovery or at all spiritual, it's one of those cultural currency things as ubiquitous as William Shatner's toupee. The first part of the prayer is asking for *the serenity to accept the things you cannot change.* I'm all for having this convo with a Higher Power, but you can also have this conversation with yourself.

And if you are a Higher Power-having person? Letting that Higher Power work through you during that conversation.

How much of your story is wrapped up in stuff over which you have zero control? And I don't mean just things other people did or circumstances that blew up in your face. I also mean your past behavior. You can't go back and change it. You can only be different now and in the future. Making amends doesn't mean decades of *mea culpas,* it means authentic regret, a real ask for forgiveness, and different behavior, followed by continued different behavior over time.

You can't change your past. You can't change other people. You can't change general life dickitude. The only control you have is over your own responses in the here-right-now. And part of that means accepting the past for what it was, learning from it (!), and moving forward. And if other people are continuing to punish you for your past dickitude that you no longer engage in…that's about their lack of ability to move on. That's okay, that's their path. And therefore it's something you cannot change.

5) Continued behavior is a choice.

If you continue to groove in the story you've been telling? If you are now conscious of your story and continue to hold on to it? *You are choosing to do so.*

Let me caveat that a bit. We humans totally have the capacity (and a likelihood) for behavioral relapse. So when we have had a particular story playing in our mind and a trauma reaction to that story, we may continue to react—in our moods and behaviors—without being aware. Especially early on in our getting over it journey. That's where we go back to Rule #4. When we find ourselves reacting, we figure out the triggers and rally the defenses for the next attack.

What I'm talking about here is continued life choices and patterns for which you know there is no happy ending. Wanting, hoping, and wishing your hopeless situation will happy-fy up in some way? This is not a Pharrell song, sorry. So continuing to date that motherfucker? Continuing to work with that shitballs boss? Continuing to try to win the affection of that disconnected parent? Not happening right now. Not with where they are in their life and their journey. So if you continue to live out that story you are doing it with intent and deliberation.

Here's the interesting part though: That's okay.

Seriously, it's okay for you to continue your behavior and make the same choices. It's your life, not mine. **But own it.** You have awareness now. I have this conversation with clients on the reg. Once we name what's going on, I ask them how long it will continue and when will they know that it's done. What's the boundary? If you are trying to make a longtime relationship work, hoping the other person will change, I can respect that. But own it as a choice you're making and figure out how long and under what circumstances you are willing to continue to do what you are doing.

6) Don't expect others to go along with you.

It's your choice, which means that it's *your* choice. It isn't fair to drag others along for the ride if they aren't willing. If your friends, family, loved ones are over something that you aren't over yet? They are allowed to be. And you really aren't allowed to get deeply butthurt over it. Yes, it would be nice to be supported. And yes, maybe you were way more supportive of them and their bullshit over the years and it would be nice for them to support your choices now.

But they aren't. And do you really want to wreck your relationship because of them being over something you aren't? Nah. Give it time. Don't bring up the situation in their presence. Let it ride out. At some point you will be able to either say "Hah! I told you so!" or invoke Carrie Fisher in *When Harry Met*

Sally with "You're right, you're right, I know you're right." Either way you didn't throw down over it in the process.

7) **Gain some perspective.**

This is the part where super-fancy actual counseling comes in. Or talking to people who you trust who will wow you with lots of truthiness about why the letting go is such a fucking *issue* for you. That's all counseling is, in the end: training and the perspective of not living that exact situation at that exact moment (plus empathy, patience, non-judgmental attitudes, and an office stocked with tissues and bottled water).

So much of what I do is connect dots, look at patterns, and offer possibilities in what I see. Maybe that would help you right now.

If nothing else? Check in with yourself for a minute. If this was your best friend in the world going through this situation, what would you tell them?

8) You are not cooking over a dung fire in Borneo. Unless you are....in which case, where did you get this zine and was it translated into Barito?)

Gaining perspective also means getting the fuck up off the pity potty if you've been sitting there for some time. And please don't misunderstand me as saying "someone always has it worse so quit your bullshit." Of course someone always has it worse. And if that was the barometer for feeling bad, that would mean that someone out there, possibly cooking over a dung fire in Borneo, has it worse than everyone else on the planet and is the only person entitled to bitch.

You are allowed to feel whateverthefuck you feel. But getting over something is far easier if you put those feelings in perspective. Is it the worst thing ever? The worst thing anyone has gone through? The worst thing *you* have gone through? If so, then give yourself the space you need to heal. If not, remind yourself that this feels bad but it's a doable thing that you can get through.

9) Grieve, FFS.

I wrote an entire zine about this, called *This Is Your Brain on Grief*. I don't need to reinvent the wheel here. If your process has a huge amount of grief associated with it, you may wanna read that one. It costs less than a latte, but fifty cents more than an Americano. So, decisions.

But as it applies here? *Getting over it* requires allowing yourself your grief process. If you haven't done the grief work, you are still holding on to *the thing*, right? Grieving is essentially a process of letting go. By holding on, you are still trying to control a situation that you cannot control. And owning that lack of control is scary shit.

Human beings are hardwired for ceremony. Consider creating one for letting go of the situation you are in. It can be whatever makes sense to you, as long as it is done with intention. There are plenty of cemeteries of bad ideas and broken relationships. It's ok to bury your own.

10) Do different shit.

There is a lot to be said for trying something new, breaking out of your groove as part of your healing process. Yes, taking a new class is pretty cool. A road trip. A vacation. Going to a Meet Up. Whatever. But it doesn't even have to be that serious. Just get the fuck out of your groove. I often encourage clients to go bring a book or their laptop to a coffee shop if they stay at home all the time. I had someone report back to me recently *"That really helped! How often is that just what people really need? To get out more?"*

We all do, really. That's the best defense against dementia. Continued learning, new stimulus, seeking novelty and the element of surprise in our lives.

If shit is so bad you are glued to the sofa right now? Try at least switching from Gilmore Girls to an interesting documentary on Netflix. Take a different route out to your mailbox. Reach out and text someone you haven't spoken to in awhile. Baby steps are fine. But try taking at least one after you put down this zine.

Any other ideas? I would seriously love to hear what has worked/is working for you in this regard. Drop me a love note (or hate mail) at theintimacydr@gmail.com

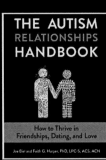

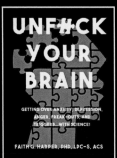
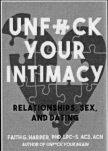